When Jesus saw the man

and knew that he had been sick

for such a long time,

Jesus asked him,

"Do you want to be well?"

JOHN 5:6 NCV

This Devotional

Is 10 Weeks of Encouragement

For ....

To Make

H E A L I N G

C H O I C E S

STEPHEN

TEN WEEKS
OF TRANSFORMING
BROKENNESS INTO
NEW LIFE

ARTERBURN

HEALING IS A CHOICE

DEVOTIONAL

COUNTRYMAN
®

NASHVILLE, TENNESSEE

10 HEALING CHOICES

GETTING STARTED

At one time or another, every human being needs healing. The type of healing required differs according to each person and their unique circumstances, but in every instance healing is a choice in which both God and man are involved. Healing is a choice. It is God's choice, and we humans can make choices to ensure we experience whatever healing God, in His eternal purpose, has for us.

This ten-week devotional—along with the other *Healing is a Choice* resources—is about your healing. It is about the disgust you have felt at whatever cruelty has been thrust upon you. It is about the isolation you have felt. It is also about the abuse or neglect you have given others. It is about the shattered dreams and lost hopes you are living with right now. It is about the big lies you've believed for so long. *Healing is a Choice* is about your healing and the choices you must make to experience the healing God has for you.

Wherever you are in your healing journey, these ten choices will help you move out of the rut you've chosen and into what God wants for your life. None of these choices are easy, but all of them can be life changing. I hope you will choose to make them. If you do, they will lead you down the path toward the healing God has for you.

Do you want to be healed? Say *yes* and read on!

~Steve

So encourage each other

and give each other strength,

just as you are doing now.

1 THESSALONIANS 5:11 NCV

THE CHOICE TO CONNECT YOUR LIFE

THE BIG LIE: *All I need to heal is just God and me.*

HEALING IS A CHOICE. It is God's choice for you, but for that healing to come, you have to choose to make a connection through the pain rather than isolate and hide because of it. Listen to some of the lies that prevent healing: "It happened a long time ago." "You are doing fine, why get help?" There are many more, but the most common of all the lies that prevent people from connecting with others or allow them to stay disconnected is the lie, "All I need is God and no one else." This lie is actually a form of denial.

Like many people, you may be willing to acknowledge that issues in your life need attention, but you deny that these issues need attention from others. You hole up in your solitary cave with God, expecting Him to meet every need and heal every pain. But that's not God's plan. His plan is for us to connect with one another to facilitate healing in our lives.

If you are like me, you would rather make it on your own. I was afraid of rejection, and I just wanted to be left alone to grieve and whine and do whatever else I wanted to do, but the faithful efforts of others kept dragging me out of the darkness and into the light of face-to-face time with other believers. The uncomfortable connection with others became the healing connection for me, and it will be the same for you. You might have some pretty good excuses to not connect with others, but God has some pretty good reasons that will overpower your excuses if you will let them. You cannot read what God has to say about connecting with each other and be convinced that He wants us to face our pain with just Him and Him alone.

The choice to connect is the first healing choice because God needs people in your life to bring about the benefits of the other choices. The other choices do no good for the hermit. You need others, and the alienation you experience in your pain blocks them off from you. So you must take a step away from your comfortable surroundings and allow others to minister to you and nurture you—no matter how difficult it is.

DAY ONE: *Look at God's truth about connecting.*

Have you made the healing choice to connect? Could the lack of connection or the superficiality of your connection be keeping you from the healing God has in store for you? If so, there is so much hope for you.

I invite you to pull out a Bible and take a moment to let God's Word sink in. Here are some Scriptures revealing that God's way is for us to work with each other and be there for each other—connected—as we seek healing. Over the next two days, look at God's truth:

- ⊰ ROMANS 12:5 tells us to depend on each other, not to just depend on God.
- ⊰ ROMANS 12:15 tells us to weep with each other, not to just weep alone.
- ⊰ ROMANS 15:14 tells us to counsel each other, not to just wait to hear from God.
- ⊰ 1 CORINTHIANS 12:25 tells us to care for each other, rather than to just receive from God.
- ⊰ 1 THESSALONIANS 5:11 tells us to encourage and edify each other, rather than to just read encouraging things from God's Word.

⊰⊱

ACT OF HEALING: Look up the verses listed above. Read them for yourself, and allow these healing truths about our connectedness to sink in.

DAY TWO: *Let God's truth live in your heart.*

Explore these verses to continue to learn about God's desire for you to connect with others:

- ⊹ EPHESIANS 4:2 tells us to uphold each other, rather than to just rely on God.

- ⊹ HEBREWS 10:24 tells us to stir up love in each other, rather than to just receive God's love.

- ⊹ 1 PETER 4:10 tells us to minister to each other, rather than to be ministered to only by the Holy Spirit.

- ⊹ JAMES 5:16 tells us to tell each other what we have done wrong, not to just tell God.

- ⊹ GALATIANS 6:2 tells us to bear each other's burdens, rather than to just trust God to take care of them.

Over and over we see the Scriptures pushing us toward each other. God encourages us to deepen our connection with others by love, devotion, confession, honor, encouragement, prayer, hospitality, submission, kindness, forgiveness, service, counsel, acceptance, and fellowship. We were born for connection—it sustains us and it heals us. Isolation is the way of the fool. Connection is the way of God.

❧

ACT OF HEALING: Memorize a verse that you found particularly helpful. Bring that verse to mind today and throughout this week as a reminder of what God is teaching you.

DAY THREE: *Remember that connecting is tough.*

The requirements of connection are tough for many of us. Not impossible, just tough. They require us to grieve the loss of some dreams, accept the reality of what is, and move toward others in spite of our pain and disappointment.

Connection also requires some selfless love: loving God even though He did not prevent pain and tragedy; loving others as God would love us; and loving ourselves because we are valuable creations of God's. This kind of love heals broken families. It lays a foundation for connection and nurtures whatever connection is there. This kind of love also motivates us to surrender to the reality that is before us.

Healing begins with a choice to surrender to God's way rather than to our own. So before we march forward on a healing path, we must be sure that we really want God's way, not our own.

We must connect with people even though they give us many excuses not to. We have to find the cracks in their walls of defense and pry them open with an honest desire for connection.

❁

ACT OF HEALING: Consider your current connections. Whom do you trust? What blocks you from connecting more with others?

DAY FOUR: *Follow Jesus' model for connection.*

Jesus showed us the necessity of connection. He spent a lot of time doing nothing but fasting and praying and connecting with God. Jesus was also connected to those around Him. He had a supportive community around Him and called on them often. In the garden the night before His death is a great example of the dual need for connection with God and others. Jesus was in deep prayer with His Father, but He wanted the others to watch and wait with Him—something they found impossible to do.

Jesus moved ahead with connection when He could have separated Himself from others. He wanted the children to come to Him. He spoke to women at wells who were "beneath" Him and involved in sin. He fellowshipped with His twelve and ate with the masses. When He sent out His disciples to reach the world, He did not send them out alone—He sent them out in twos, connected to each other. We would do well to follow the example of Christ's repeated displays of the need for connection.

❦

ACT OF HEALING: Connect with Jesus in intense prayer today. Ask Him to teach you how to connect meaningfully with others and to give you guidance in making the best human connections.

DAY FIVE: *Choose the rewards of connection.*

When you decide to connect, you decide to live life as God intended it. His very existence, the Trinity, is a model of relationship. He designed the family, which is a collection of relationships. His church exists and builds His kingdom while in relationship. He ordained marriage as the ultimate relationship between a man and a woman. So when the barriers come down, and you reach for connection, you start to experience life as God intended. Although you might be uncomfortable, you start to come alive as you seek deeper levels of connection with those around you.

Connection allows us to feel accepted. This is healing to the soul in a way we would never know if we stayed alone. There is relief when we connect. It fills in the gaps and provides the missing pieces because our makeup is aligned toward connection with others. It allows us to move to the heights of emotions, feeling love, joy, and hope.

⚜

ACT OF HEALING: Think of someone with whom you really connect. Tell that person how much he or she means to you. Thank that person for being there for you, and remind that person that you're there to support them, too.

DAY SIX: *Recognize that connecting starts with God,*
but it doesn't stop there.

The choice to heal through connections starts with our connection with God. We build this connection through the study of God's Word, meditation, and prayer. As we live more to please Him, we experience a growing awareness of His presence and an intimate connection that takes us through the toughest of times with hope and the best of times with divine joy.

Connection with God is vital, but it is not enough. We must branch out from a "God only" mentality and reach out to others. In humility we can begin a new level of connection with others that is essential to the healing process. Healing communities such as healthy churches, support groups, and recovery programs become the healing foundation upon which all other choices are made and played out. Go no further before you stop and choose to connect with God. Then take a healing risk and connect with others who can help you heal and experience life to the fullest.

❦

ACT OF HEALING: Spend some time in prayer and meditation today as you prepare to make connections with others an active part of your healing.

DAY SEVEN: *Allow nothing to stand in the way.*

Whatever you can do to connect, do it. Face-to-face connection is the richest form of connection, but if the only way you can get outside of your house is through the Internet, then find some safe groups to connect with online. Don't let any limitation be an excuse not to connect. Attempt to build a community with different levels of connection. At one end of the connection spectrum is mere support, where you can count on others to be there for you when you need them. They encourage and comfort in times of need. At the other end of the spectrum is true intimacy, where there is the sharing of the deepest parts of who you are. In this intimacy, you feel a bond, an inseverable link that strengthens with time; as you grow, you develop many levels of intimacy through humor, history, shared dreams, and common joys. This level of communication provides the richest life possible.

❧

ACT OF HEALING: Connect with God; then connect with one of His children today. Make a phone call, write a note, or send an e-mail. Take action to connect with others today.

BE CAREFUL WITH BOUNDARIES

Our tendency is to do anything but connect. We tend to isolate and we do it in some very subtle ways. Dr. Henry Cloud and Dr. John Townsend, my good friends and colleagues, wrote a groundbreaking book titled *Boundaries*. Many people have found hope and healing because of it. In *Boundaries*, Henry and John help readers make some tough choices that often result in people getting back their lives. They help people establish what they are entitled to in relationships and what to do when someone inappropriately crosses a boundary. This insight is extremely meaningful to victims of abuse or people with so little self-esteem that they don't know when to say "no." But for every good use of a boundary, there is a misuse of the concept that allows some people to remain disconnected.

One of the misuses of the boundaries concept occurs when an isolated and disconnected person puts up a wall in the name of a boundary. He builds a wall rather than staking out the territory of his identity. In the name of protecting himself, he encases himself in an impenetrable bunker where his emotions are protected and his secrets are secure. Soon he builds four solid walls and bolts them shut. This becomes a casket that he lives inside—protected, guarded, but dead.

Every person who has ever set a boundary must ask if it was a healthy boundary or an unhealthy wall. Did it lead to healthier connection or prevent connection from taking place? If it is the latter, the first task of healing is to tear down that wall. Remove the barriers between you and others, and then engage in a healthy relationship that may indeed hurt you in the "normal" ways sometimes, but it won't allow you to exist in a semi-comatose state.

There are many ways we live out the lie that we must protect ourselves from all people. One way is to lead others while we keep our distance. Or we cling to others so tightly that they fight to keep their distance from us. Or we spew out an exhibitionist confession that pushes people away from us. All of these are connection killers when what we need is real and true and deep connection. We find this type of connection in mutuality by sharing ourselves and wanting to share the experience of others.

We must listen, receive, and have empathy while at the same time giving, contributing, and reaching for the hearts of others. When we do, life opens up before us in ways we never knew possible. If single, we learn that we can connect without sex and that sex prevents us from experiencing God's plan for connection and love. If we are married, stable and set, but disconnected, we can step into a new level of intimacy with our spouses when we go to work on our connection. Wherever we are in life, we can move closer to others as we move closer to God.

By helping each other

with your troubles,

you truly obey the law of Christ.

GALATIANS 6:2 NCV

The Lord GOD has put his Spirit in me,

because the LORD has appointed me

to tell the good news to the poor.

He has sent me to comfort

those whose hearts are broken,

to tell the captives they are free,

and to tell the prisoners they are released.

He has sent me to announce the time

when the LORD will show his kindness

and the time when our God

will punish evil people.

He has sent me to comfort

all those who are sad.

ISAIAH 61:1–2 NCV

WEEK TWO:

THE CHOICE TO FEEL YOUR LIFE

THE BIG LIE: *Real Christians should have a real peace in all circumstances.*

Not many people see pain as a gift from God, but it is. In fact, it is at the point of pain that we often question God. There is a common belief that if He is real and if He loves us, then He will keep pain from us. Most of us hate pain, and we do everything we can to avoid it, and rightfully so—by its very nature, pain hurts. If we are healthy and wise we make the best decisions possible that will lead to the least amount of pain in our lives. Other people do foolish things that cause great emotional pain and then rather than feel it, they deny it, drown it out with booze, suppress it with food, or whisk it away with a sexual encounter. They mask the pain and try to remove it rather than deal with its source. In the process they question God's presence and power because of all the pain they have produced in their own lives. They often will view pain as a curse rather than as a gift.

Ashlyn Blocker's life dramatically demonstrates that pain is a special gift from God that protects us. Ashlyn cannot feel pain. Her parents knew there was something wrong when she placed her hand on a hot pressure washer and felt nothing. Ashlyn stood there, stared at her red and blistered hand, but did not cry, and her mother knew they had a problem. When her baby teeth came in, Ashlyn would wake up with swollen and bloody lips from chewing on them in her sleep. While eating she unknowingly bites through her tongue. Her food has to be cooled because she cannot tell if it is too hot. They place ice cubes in hot soup to prevent the scalding of her mouth. Ashlyn's mother, Tara Blocker, said: "Some people would say that's a good thing. But no, it's not. Pain's there for a reason. It lets your body know something's wrong and it needs to be fixed. I'd give anything for her to feel pain."

What is true of physical pain and the body is true for emotional pain and the soul. Pain is a gift from God to let us know that something is not right, that something in our life needs attention and fixing.

When we feel our lives, we are tuned in to pain as it emerges and can resolve it before our lives begin to revolve around it. But if we are not allowed to or if we choose not to feel the pain, we will add hurt on top of injury and inflict further difficulty and conflict on our lives, just like the little girl who continued to injure herself. Pain is a gift. It is not one we actively seek, but when it appears in our lives, we need to react appropriately, rather than deny or neglect it.

DAY ONE: *Reflect on Jesus' sorrow.*

The prophet Isaiah said Jesus would be a man who experienced sorrow (Isaiah 53:3). We read of Jesus' experience in the Garden of Gethsemane, just before His crucifixion (Matthew 26). We hear Him ask His disciples to watch and wait with Him because He was so deeply troubled. He felt emotional pain to such a degree that He sweated drops of blood. Sweating blood only comes from feeling the deepest of pain, suffering, and sorrow. He was in the midst of great despair even in—and especially during—times of intense prayer with His Father. This was God as man, who today knows your emotional pain because He experienced it while on this earth. He did not minimize it or "superficialize" it. He felt it to the core of His soul.

Jesus knew the final outcome. He could see the marvelous result of His suffering. No one needed to tell Him that He would save souls by the millions. But He still had to work things out with His Father.

❈

ACT OF HEALING: Read Isaiah 53:3 and Matthew 26. Meditate on the significance of knowing that Jesus can identify with the pain you feel.

DAY TWO: *Recognize the transforming power of pain.*

Our emotions are gifts from God. Paul showed us that good can come from experiencing bad feelings:

> *I am no longer sorry that I sent that letter to you, though I was sorry for a time, for I know that it was painful to you for a little while. Now I am glad I sent it, not because it hurt you, but because the pain caused you to have remorse and change your ways. It was the kind of sorrow God wants his people to have, so you were not harmed by us in any way. For God can use sorrow in our lives to help us turn away from sin and seek salvation.* (2 CORINTHIANS 7:8–10 NLT)

The sorrowful feelings led to making things right. Glossing over them or pushing them down or not expressing them would have eliminated a great opportunity for change and transformation.

❦

ACT OF HEALING: Ask God to show you any feelings you have been trying to ignore and to help you understand what those feelings mean. Let Him begin to use those feelings to bring transformation to your life.

DAY THREE: *Be willing to die to yourself.*

We need to die to self, rather than trying to drown out our emotions or kill our feelings. The choice to heal means that rather than eat a carton of ice cream when we are anxious, we die to the urge to binge, feel the anxiety, live in it, discover its source, and then resolve it and experience a new level of healing. The choice to heal is the choice not to take a drink at the point of anger and rage; it is looking at the anger and rage as a sign that something is wrong and must be addressed. We live in the anger, experience it, explore it, and find out what is at the heart of it, until we finally resolve it in order to heal our lives. We experience the feelings—dying to our selfish urges to delay them, bury them, or smother them—and then we use those feelings as a signal that we must do more work to clean out the emotional baggage from the darkest parts of our souls.

❦

ACT OF HEALING: Reflect on the following questions: How do you try to drown your feelings? What does it mean to die to yourself? What feelings do you need to embrace today?

DAY FOUR: *Refuse to believe the big lie.*

Many are living the big lie that if we are real Christians we should experience a real peace in all circumstances. The lie only serves to delay the pain that must be experienced as a gift from God. The gift of pain pierces us, and we instantly know we have a problem to solve or a mystery to unravel. When someone we love dies, we have a problem to solve. We must find a way to live without that person. We have to exist without their daily touch or frequent contact, encouragement, or nurturing. If we deny that pain, we don't solve the problem.

The lie of instant peace can lead us to constant and ongoing pain that will not die until we feel it, express it, understand it, and resolve it. The big lie prevents us from healing. It moves us into superficiality and fake connection. Feeling our lives and the pain in them allows us to connect in authentic and intimate ways.

❦

ACT OF HEALING: List any areas of your life in which you have tried to feel "instant peace" instead of real emotions. Let yourself feel the pain so you can heal.

DAY FIVE: *Invite quiet reflection.*

Today might be a good day to do a pain inventory and a feelings checkup. Perhaps you could find the time to get away, be still, and quiet your mind. If you do, ask yourself these questions:

- ⧫ What am I afraid of?
- ⧫ What is missing?
- ⧫ Am I empty?
- ⧫ What am I filling up on?
- ⧫ Why am I refusing to feel?
- ⧫ What feelings am I avoiding?

When you take this kind of inventory you might find that you can see a pattern of protection from the painful feelings you need to address. You may find yourself hiding from pain and hiding from other people. You might see a tremendous amount of defensiveness on your part, and you might find yourself isolated and alone.

❈

ACT OF HEALING: Spend time reflecting on these questions, and take a few minutes to write your answers. Talk with God about what you wrote.

DAY SIX: *Face feelings of anger and guilt.*

In a quiet place and with a quiet mind you may find the answers to questions you did not even know you were avoiding. You might find some areas that are sensitive and need resolution. You may discover that feeling your life is not something to avoid. You may find it quite bearable in the bad times and very enjoyable in the good times.

Yesterday you explored feelings of pain and fear. Continue in quiet reflection today as you consider these questions:

- ⊰ Do I hold a grudge?
- ⊰ Am I angry because I feel controlled?
- ⊰ Is my past in my present because of anger toward someone who hurt me?
- ⊰ Am I seeking revenge in any form?

Now take a look at the guilt and shame you bear:

- ⊰ Am I feeling guilty about a current habit?
- ⊰ Do I experience shame from something someone did to me?
- ⊰ Am I knowingly involved in a sin?
- ⊰ When I feel guilt, am I shutting it down with food or drink?

❧

ACT OF HEALING: Resolve to take action to deal with one area you have identified that is troubling you. Identify a step toward healing, and then act on it.

DAY SEVEN: *Trust Jesus for your healing.*

When you put your trust in Jesus, your life becomes manageable, and your state of mind becomes enjoyable because your feelings are not raging out of control. You don't have to worry about anything when you trust God for everything (Matthew 6:25). There is no reason to be anxious about anything when you have placed your trust in God (Philippians 4:6). When you live this way you are at peace with the world and yourself, and you are free to make the connections you need to make. You are free to feel the emptiness, the fear, and the anger because you know you will survive. You know that in the end all of these feelings will be resolved and in the hands of God, so every day you can turn over to Him a little bit more than the day before. You can feel your life and experience your life to the fullest

ACT OF HEALING: Over the next week, keep a record of the feelings you experience. Pray about each emotion as you write it down, and ask God to reveal the source and lead you on His path toward transformation.

Those who are sad now are happy,
because God will comfort them.

MATTHEW 5:4 NCV

People with understanding

want more knowledge,

but fools

just want more foolishness.

PROVERBS 15:14 NCV

THE CHOICE TO INVESTIGATE YOUR LIFE IN SEARCH OF TRUTH

THE BIG LIE: *It does no good to look back or look inside.*

Are you doing things that separate you from others and from the life you could be enjoying? Do you wish areas of your life that are full of conflict and struggle would just go away? Have you ever walked away from a conversation or even a fight wondering why you did what you did or said what you said? Almost everyone has, but not everyone goes through the pain and struggle of getting to the "why" behind the choices that cause problems, conflict, and emotional turmoil. We heal our lives as we search for truth about why we do what we do and why we feel the way we feel.

All of us have mysteries inside of us that need to be solved. In the situations above, when the mysteries are solved, there is an opportunity for the relationship to be healed. Insight and awareness lead to informed choices that can heal, but if no one ever stops to consider the "why" behind the actions or the feelings that lead to the actions, there is little hope for change or healing. It would be helpful for all of us to stop and take a look at life in the past, where we are today, and where it is all leading to in the future. The Bible challenges us to take a look inside: "Let us examine our ways" (Lamentations 3:40 NIV). Our ways are our habits, conflicts, character defects, and the patterns in our relationships. When we are willing to take a look, we discover some areas that need work so healing may begin.

There is a mystery of the mind to solve when you come to the end of yourself and feel as if you cannot go on. You can give up, or you can hold on and allow yourself more time to solve the mystery that leads to your sense of being overwhelmed, alone, and desperate.

There is a mystery to solve when you lose something you hoped to keep. You can just move on, or you can investigate why it meant so much to you and how you lost it. Solve that mystery and you may find that you won't lose so much in the future.

It is important that you discover the truth about you. Perhaps that is why you started this book and are still reading. You really do want to learn and allow that insight to lead to healing. Maybe you have suffered a severe blow and are trying to recover from a divorce or a death or a loss of a job or something even more traumatic. Perhaps you are tired of not healing from some abuse in your past. Sexual, emotional, or physical abuse may still influence too much of what you do, and you are ready for healing. If you are, you have to look within and discover some things about yourself that are not so pleasant. You have to solve the mystery of why some people who have been abused move on, while you have become stuck. Are you willing to investigate? Don't you want to know what it is within you that either drives you or is driving you crazy? Wouldn't you like to identify some of the destructive patterns you have developed and change them for good? If so, let's take a look.

God, examine me and know my heart;

test me and know my nervous thoughts.

See if there is any bad thing in me.

Lead me on the road to everlasting life.

PSALM 139:23-24 NCV

DAY ONE: *Prepare to open up your life.*

Every person has blind spots, not just foggy spots. Foggy spots are those spots where we are unclear. We know they are there but we just can't quite grasp them or banish them. Blind spots are different—blind spots are areas we do not see at all. We are not in denial about blind spots because we don't even know they are there.

You may think you are fully aware of all aspects of your being, but you are not. Some areas of your life have mysteries that you cannot solve on your own because you do not see the problem. You are completely blind to the reality of what is there, and the only way you will be able to "see" is with the help of others. But first, before you ask for help with what you *don't* see, take a look at what you *do* see. Open yourself up with your own scalpel and take a look.

❁

ACT OF HEALING: Pray a simple prayer today asking the Lord to make you willing to look at yourself honestly and deal with what you see.

DAY TWO: *Take inventory of your life.*

Take the time to hold your life up to the light of truth and see what is there. Following are several questions that will aid in taking inventory of your life:

- ⊰ Starting as early as you can remember, who hurt you? How?

- ⊰ What was your reaction to being hurt? Did you forgive the people who hurt you, hold a grudge, or try to seek your own revenge?

- ⊰ Is there any way you could have altered your reaction to being hurt?

- ⊰ Starting as early as you can remember, whom did you hurt?

- ⊰ Did they do something first that hurt you, or were you acting without provocation?

- ⊰ What was your reaction when you realized you had hurt someone?

- ⊰ What have you done to rectify the problems of when you were hurt and when you hurt others?

❧

ACT OF HEALING: Write out your answers to the questions above. If you get stuck on certain questions, take a break and work on these questions over the span of a few days.

DAY THREE: *Continue the inventory.*

Continue to learn about yourself today as you explore your strengths and weaknesses.

- Are you aware of your five greatest *strengths?* Write down what you think they are, and then ask five other people to tell you what they think they are.

- Are you aware of your five greatest *weaknesses?* Write down what you think they are, and then ask five other people to tell you what they think they are.

- What have you done to misuse your strengths? Have you been a good steward of them or have you wasted them?

- What have you done to use your strengths well? Ask the same five people as in the previous questions where they have seen you use them well.

- What have you done to correct or work on your weaknesses?

- What could you do to work on them? Make a list.

❦

ACT OF HEALING: Ask someone close to you to be your partner in truth. Ask that person to give you honest feedback about yourself so you can continue to work on the areas that need help.

DAY FOUR: *Share with at least one other person.*

Take what you have learned about yourself and share it with another person who loves you, is wise, keeps confidences, and is committed to helping you become the best person you can be. Tell that person that you want honest feedback. Let him or her know that there are no points off for truth—you can handle the truth—and invite that person to share it with you.

As you go through life you want to be sure that at least one other person has heard you confess your sins and shortcomings. You need to be sure that at least one other person has heard your full story—warts and all. You also need to be sure that at least one other person on this planet is allowed to tell you the truth about yourself.

❧

ACT OF HEALING: Share your full story—warts and all—with the person you have asked to be your partner in truth. Invite this person to share hard truths with you, and commit to openly receiving that feedback.

DAY FIVE: *Pray with another person.*

In addition to your being able to share with one other person, you also need to be sure that at least one other person is praying for you. Satan is real, and supernatural warfare is going on right now. Prayer is a supernatural means of fighting the enemy who wants nothing less than the complete worst for you. Find a person, through your church or the Internet or through friends, who has a strong prayer life, and ask that person to pray for you as you search for the truth about yourself. Make certain that you also are praying. Pray that God will reveal all things to you that you need to know to grow more like Him. Prayer is a supernatural tool to uncover the blind spots and begin to grow.

❦

ACT OF HEALING: Find a person who will commit to praying for you faithfully. Don't be shy—people want to help you and will be glad you asked! Try to find this prayer partner by the end of the week.

DAY SIX: *Throw off your encumbrances.*

The big lie that you might use or that others might tell you is that you should never look back or look inside. Hebrews 12:1 admonishes us to throw off any encumbrance that would weigh us down and prevent us from achieving what God has called us to do. Don't listen to the big lie. If you are riddled with guilt, shame, remorse, anger, rage, anxiety, or fear from your past, you need to do some work to solve the mystery of why these feelings exist.

These things are the encumbrances or the burdens you need to throw off. Do it before you miss one more day of living as God would have you live. Do the work, and don't listen to anyone who would tell you it is destructive. Become the best student of yourself. Know yourself so that you can come to know all that God has planned for you and so you can live within that plan.

❧

ACT OF HEALING: What encumbrances do you need to throw off? List them and commit to the Lord that you will do the work necessary to get rid of them.

DAY SEVEN: *Break through your limitations.*

Most of us want to believe we can break through our denial, shine a light on all of our blind spots, and develop new insights into ourselves without the messiness of working with someone else. The truth is that someone else must help you. I have suggested that you get help from a trusted friend, but sometimes it requires more than a layperson's experience to help you see where you need to make changes.

Helping your life by getting treatment might be the most important step taken. We will explore that choice in week five, but before then some additional work in feeling and investigating your life could set you free to heal. As you have explored the truth about yourself you might have uncovered some ungrieved losses. Next week we will look at the importance of grief in the healing process.

❦

ACT OF HEALING: Ask God to prepare you for the next steps in the healing process, whatever they may be. Ask Him to show you any ungrieved losses and to give you a willingness to pursue any avenue that will bring you to wholeness.

Confess your sins to each other

and pray for each other so

God can heal you.

When a believing person prays,

great things happen.

JAMES 5:16 NCV

I tell you the truth,

you will cry and be sad,

but the world will be happy.

You will be sad, but

your sadness will become joy.

JOHN 16:20 NCV

WEEK FOUR:

THE CHOICE TO HEAL YOUR FUTURE

THE BIG LIE: *Time heals all wounds.*

All of us have had dreams sputter and die. We've all been wounded by pain, disappointment, and loss. I have talked to and worked with people who have lived for decades in the pain of shattered dreams and broken expectations. They are still suffering at fifty or sixty because of something that happened when they were a child or a teenager; the pain is still working on them, eating at them, and robbing them of the life they could have. But I'm going to invite you to heal your future.

The Bible advises not to worry about tomorrow because tomorrow has enough trouble on its own. Once it arrives, tomorrow could be full of more trouble than today, so don't bring that trouble into your life ahead of time (Matthew 6:34). It is great and godly advice to not worry about your future, but it is also good advice to heal your future so that tomorrow will have as few problems as possible. Some people never stop to think about how they might heal or fix their future, and there are some practical ways to make your future the best possible. The Bible points to the ant for a lesson in healing your future:

> *Take a lesson from the ants, you lazybones. Learn from their ways and be wise! Even though they have no prince, governor, or ruler to make them work, they labor hard all summer, gathering food for the winter.* (PROVERBS 6:6–8 NLT)

Someone might read that and say that the ant was a bit worried about winter. Knowing the reality of something and preparing for it—doing the work—is not worry. A way for the ant to heal his future winter is through preparation and making provision, or he can infect his future with laziness that will result in an empty stomach and death. It is during the harvest season that the ant chooses to take healing action that will heal the winter. Every person can do the same thing in their own lives.

We can make the coming years more secure by saving money. We can enrich our future by building strong relationships that will last a lifetime and beyond. We can grow a loving family that will nurture us in the twilight of our lives. We can plant some healing seeds that will produce a harvest of peace and serenity. Grieving also heals our future; doing the tough work of grieving prepares the soil for a healthy harvest of connected relationships and for living a life with purpose and meaning. When we grieve we come right alongside Jesus, follow His example, and do exactly what He did.

DAY ONE: *Identify your dreams and hurts.*

Think about your great dreams that haven't come true. Did you believe that you would grow up, easily discover whom God chose for you, marry that person, make a lot of money, have great kids who were never a problem, and then just continue to live happily ever after? Was your dream to be a star of the stage or screen? Were you told you had great talent and you should go for it and make it to the top? Was your dream to live a peaceful life teaching at a university with the security of tenure, writing bestseller after bestseller? Did you have big dreams that never came true?

Many people have stopped dreaming because they have been hurt so badly they don't believe dreams come true. You may be one of those who was abused or neglected as a child, and that pain is still influencing who you are today. You may have been hurt because someone close to you died. It's time to reexamine the disappointments and pain that cloud your days.

❦

ACT OF HEALING: What were your dreams for your life that never came true? Tell God and another close friend about those unfulfilled dreams.

DAY TWO: *Know that Jesus was acquainted with grief.*

Jesus was "a Man of sorrows and acquainted with grief" (Isaiah 53:3 NKJV). That presents the question: what would make Him grieve? Perhaps it was the loss of a perfect world. Perhaps He grieved the loss of the position He surrendered in order to put on an earthsuit, come live as we live, and die for us.

Knowing that Jesus walked where we walk gives me comfort and courage at the same time. I can share in His suffering, and I can bond with Him as I go through the grief process. I can be confident that He knows how to comfort me, because He has been there and experienced it all. I also can rest assured that grieving is the right thing to do. If we were called to be full of happy talk all the time and have smiles on our faces all the time, then I do not think Jesus would have been termed "a Man of sorrows and acquainted with grief."

❦

ACT OF HEALING: Write out and meditate on Isaiah 53:3. Thank Jesus that He understands what you are going through.

DAY THREE: *Trade your emotions.*

"I tell you the truth, you will weep and mourn while the world rejoices. You will grieve, but your grief will turn to joy" (John 16:20 NLT). Joy waits on the other side of grief. Grieving is a decision to heal your future and replace your pain with joy. You trade the nagging, persistent pain of your daily life for a deep, sharp pain that dredges out the emotional waste of your life and leaves you free to experience joy. Whatever you're grieving, the pain of the grieving time removes the curse of future pain. Your pain is resolved and no longer needs to be fed.

The losses and the feeling of living a life of "less than" are traded for the gains and the freedom that come from living through the reality of loss. The feeling of disconnected alienation is traded for a sense of connection, belonging, and community. Dependency on your own resources and survival tactics is traded for a trust in God and a dependency on Him and His way.

ACT OF HEALING: Memorize John 16:20, and allow it to encourage you when you fear that there is no end to your grief.

DAY FOUR: *Tear down your walls.*

We try to protect ourselves from more pain when we don't fully experience our grief. We arrange our lives so that we will not have to endure more pain than we can bear, and we defend our ground by not allowing others to speak truth into our lives. But with the losses grieved, we are more willing to listen and hear the truth. We are no longer living on the "edge of overwhelmed," so we allow people to connect with us at deeper levels. We notice that we are able to live through the vulnerability of connection.

We also begin to notice that we have less and less need to present ourselves as something other than who we really are. We stop putting up walls of pretense. We have no need to hide behind the old façades that protected us from hurt but prevented us from knowing the life God had for us.

✺

ACT OF HEALING: Can you recall a recent situation in which you reacted defensively or put up a wall of pretense? Think about the source of your response. Resolve not to hide behind that façade.

DAY FIVE: *Reject the lie that "time heals all wounds."*

The big lie is that time will heal your deep wounds. It actually does just the opposite. Time seems to infect the wounds that are already there. The longer we live with them the greater their damage. Instead of just time, we need time that is well-spent resolving our pasts and healing our wounds.

How you mark your time can be the most powerful healing choice you can make. If you want time to be healing, seek out the places where healing occurs and spend your time there doing the work required. Refuse to believe or live in the lie that mere time is going to heal you. Time will fade the pain and lighten your despair, but it will not heal you. Stop just waiting for time to heal you. Instead, find a healing community where you can grieve your losses and unfulfilled expectations, let go of them, and grab onto the life that is available.

❧

ACT OF HEALING: Connect with someone close to you today. Spend time talking or praying with that person, or make plans to get together in the near future.

Day Six: *Embrace God's cleansing power.*

When *who we want to be* and *who we pretend to be* are stripped away, we see simply *who we are*, and we discover that who we are is enough. We are created uniquely and wonderfully with all of what we need. We mess that up sometimes, and others also attempt to mess it up for us, but grief is a cleansing power that takes care of the mess, no matter where it originated. The psalmist said, "I weep with grief; my heart is heavy with sorrow" (Psalm 119:28 TLB). He was not just shedding tears; he was cleansing his life of the past. He was healing his future. He was letting go of *what was* and *what might have been* and reaching instead for *what is* and *what is to be*.

❀

ACT OF HEALING: Whom do you believe that God has created you to be? Reflect on the life you believe God intends for you, and accept that who you are is enough.

DAY SEVEN: *Let go.*

Do you need to let go? Do you need to fall back in the arms of God and allow Him to heal you? Do you need to express your feelings and protest to Him? Do you need to ask Him for power to let go? If you do, and if you persevere with Him, He will grant you the power to let go because healing is what He desires for your heart (Isaiah 61:1).

Healing is a choice. It is God's choice, but we can make choices that allow the healing He has for us to be manifested in our lives. Healing is a choice to let go of our past hurts by grieving them, and grieving is a choice to heal the future.

❦

ACT OF HEALING: Spend time in prayer. Ask God to give you the strength to let go of the past so that you can embrace the future He wants you to have.

His anger lasts only a moment, but his kindness lasts for a lifetime. Crying may last for a night, but joy comes in the morning.

PSALM 30:5 NCV

Plans fail without good advice,

but they succeed

with the advice of many others.

Proverbs 15:22 NCV

WEEK FIVE:

THE CHOICE TO HELP
YOUR LIFE

THE BIG LIE: *I can figure this out by myself.*

I am all for us feeling good about ourselves and being grateful for the gifts that God has given us. I am amazed at His wonderful creations that we call *man* and *woman*. Our brains alone are beyond my ability to comprehend; the more I learn about computers, the more amazed I am at the one living inside my head. I am all for building ourselves up with positive self-talk about how great a creation we are and how marvelously talented we are. Those are really nice things for us to do, but in the midst of our happy talk, we need to accept the glaring reality that each of us, to some degree or another, has a sick mind. Its wiring and chemistry might be functioning perfectly, but it is functioning in the human state of perpetual sickness that takes us down paths we neither want nor need to travel.

Right in front of every person is a path that is very wide and easy to follow (Proverbs 14:12). As far down that path as you can see, it seems to be a very pleasant and pleasurable way to go. You end up in the midst of death and destruction, however, when you take that path to where you want to go. That path is not the path of truth, it is not the path of wisdom, and it is not the path of God. It is the path of the sick mind.

The mind we use to do so much is defective. It is so sick that microbiologists end up delivering mail. Pastors end up selling stocks and bonds. Married men end up in relationships with prostitutes. Women end up living like doormats. Geniuses end up behind bars. Wealthy people shoplift. Healthy people gain 180 pounds. Mothers hit the children they love. Fathers molest the children they always dreamed of treating better than they were treated. Teachers end up selling insurance. Counselors end up in inappropriate relationships with those they wanted to help. Fun and exciting people end up bolted to the security of their own homes, unable to walk out their front doors. The sick mind does all this and more.

People can watch their lives fall apart. They can experience confusion and hopelessness for years, and yet still believe that they must and will find a way to help themselves. Perhaps they have heard the term "self-help" and think that a lot of people succeed because they have figured out how to help themselves. Nothing could be further from the truth.

Self-help is not really self help at all. Self-help that really helps is God help, it is group help, it is expert help. It is anything but a person's sick mind finally finding the path to a great and wonderful life. The sick mind that leads us down the wrong path is not going to somehow find the right path one day. In order to find that path we must seek help beyond ourselves. We must reach out and find the treatment that we need.

The teaching of a wise person gives life.

It is like a fountain
that can save people from death.

PROVERBS 13:14 NCV

DAY ONE: *Identify the barriers to getting help.*

If you saw a dog on the side of the road that was wounded or sick, you probably would help that dog. If you would do that for a stray animal, why wouldn't you do it for yourself?

You might be embarrassed to seek help; it would be a sign of weakness for you to walk into a counselor's office or attend a Celebrate Recovery group. You would be "found out," and the last thing you want is for someone to know you have a problem. So you protect your problem and your image, but you ruin your life in the process. At least you prevent your real life from beginning. Rather than admit a limitation or allow anyone to know that part of you is broken, you continue the masquerade and avoid any place people go to get help. You may view the decision not to get help as rational, but it is part of the denial that a sick mind needs to stay in sickness.

❈

ACT OF HEALING: Have you ever considered getting help in the past? List the fears or reservations that may have prevented you from doing so.

DAY TWO: *Stop deceiving yourself.*

If you see a person struck by a hit-and-run driver, you don't listen to the person tell you they will be all right, that they just need a minute to get themselves together. You see the severity of the injury. The hurt person is in denial or shock. It is no different for the person limping past the counselor's office or the pastor's suite or the recovery group while saying to himself or herself, "I am going to be just fine." If that wounded person is you, then pull over, reach out, and get the help you need.

This condition of self-deception is addressed quite plainly in Proverbs 3:5–8. The passage directs you not to lean on your own understanding. Do not fool yourself into thinking you have the answers and will figure things out. This passage is an admonition to move out of your own understanding and seek help and insight from someone else who may be able to help you with the deep wounds that must be treated.

❦

ACT OF HEALING: Meditate on Proverbs 3:5–8 today. Ask yourself: In what ways am I deceiving myself? Do I need to seek outside help for my untreated wounds?

DAY THREE: *Find wise counsel.*

Reaching out to get the help you need does not come only in the form of a recovery group or a counselor's office. Many times the help you need can be found at the local church, but for it to be effective you need to participate in that church in other ways, too. Wise pastors can perceive things you might not. But your life has to be open and available to those pastors. They have to know you through your involvement in community with them. Are you listening to a pastor? Are you responsive to what the pastor says? Or are you still running your own recovery and healing show? A pastor might be just what the Great Physician ordered to treat what ails you, if you seek the help and are responsive to it.

※

ACT OF HEALING: Are you involved in a local church? If not, take a step toward finding one today. If you are involved in a church, consider meeting with your pastor or becoming more involved in your church community.

DAY FOUR: *Seek treatment.*

When you want to be healed and are willing to go to any extreme to find healing, treatment becomes an option. When you accept that your home remedies do not work, treatment becomes something you seek out rather than have forced upon you. You're ready to step out of your isolation and seek the help of someone outside of yourself.

The goal of treatment is to RISE above your problems rather than be controlled and dominated by them. Right now whatever you are dealing with might seem like a vulture hovering over your head or perched on your shoulder. You cannot do anything without being aware of that huge presence dominating your thoughts. The goal of treatment would be to shrink that vulture into the size of a gnat. You would know it was still there, but it would not be in control. It would no longer be the dominating force in your life.

❦

ACT OF HEALING: Consider what issues in your life feel like a vulture hovering over you. Visualize those issues shrinking to the size of a gnat, and consider how treatment can help get you to that point.

DAY FIVE: *R.I.S.E.*

R I S E is an acronym that summarizes the benefits of treatment and gives some direction in what to do while you participate in treatment:

R ⊣ Reduce the stress in your life by learning new management skills. Reduce conflicts that cause inner turmoil and difficulties in your relationships. Reduce the negative patterns that have set in over your lifetime. Reduce the substances you use to help cope with the pain in your life.

I ⊣ Increase your self-awareness and how you affect people who interact with you. Increase the healthy influences in your life.

S ⊣ Substitute positive emotions for negative ones. Substitute the willingness to risk for fear. Substitute humility for arrogance. Substitute acceptance for anger. Substitute peace for anxiety. Substitute surrender for control.

E ⊣ Eliminate addictive behaviors. Eliminate a critical and judgmental spirit. Eliminate repetitive sins in your life.

❧

ACT OF HEALING: Which areas listed above would be particularly important in your healing process? Take a few minutes to journal about them.

DAY SIX: *Investigate your options.*

You might think of psychological or psychiatric treatment as the only way to get help, but there are many other forms of help, too. You might need medication to help you think clearly or feel appropriately. A psychologist or a licensed marriage and family therapist can provide counseling or therapy. A pastor who is trained in counseling may be the perfect resource for one-to-one therapy. Group therapy involving others with similar problems may help you uncover areas within yourself that need work.

Some of the most helpful treatments don't come from a trained professional. There are many options outside of a professional's office that don't cost anything and have been used by thousands for transformation and healing. Support groups such as Alcoholics Anonymous or Al-Anon meet all around the world. Celebrate Recovery is a growing Christian resource that already can be found in about three thousand churches. Anyone who struggles in some area should locate a group specific to their struggle and at least give it a try.

❧

ACT OF HEALING: Spend some time investigating your options for help through your church or community. Finding out what is available is the next step toward healing.

DAY SEVEN: *Admit that you don't have the answers.*

In a Gatorade commercial, athletes drink the orange or green beverage, work up a huge sweat, and orange or green sweat beads pop out everywhere. Then comes the question, "Is it in you?" When it comes to the answers for fixing your life, the answer is "No." The sick mind that led you down the path of sickness will not lead you to a place of health. You will have to reach beyond what is in your head and reach out for the help you need.

You may have been telling yourself the big lie that you can figure things out on your own. I don't think so. I think that if you could do it alone, you would have done so by now. You have not because you cannot. Although you might see that as a weakness, the greatest act of strength you can exhibit is to admit you don't have the answer within you and to turn to someone who does.

※

ACT OF HEALING: If you haven't yet, decide today to commit to a plan of treatment. If you have already taken this step, take stock of where you are and where you are going. Make that commitment to a treatment plan more real by vocalizing it to a close friend.

Listen to advice and

accept correction,

and in the end

you will be wise.

Proverbs 19:20 NCV

THE SOONER THE BETTER

❧

If your sick mind is causing you distress, the sooner you get help for it the better. In the meantime, your body is harming itself, including harming your mind. In *Newsweek*, September 27, 2004, there was an excellent sidebar by Josh Ulick on page forty-six. He explained how the body can harm itself if we do not relieve our conflicts and the problems of our past. The problem comes from our inborn ability to spring into action when there is great danger. A chemical reaction occurred that set the body into action when a caveman perceived a threat. That was good for him, but it is not so good for us if we do not see the problem and respond to it properly.

Today, rather than having supernatural strength "to kill the rhino," we sit and stew in our own juices because for us there is no rhino. When the body senses a threat, it gets ready for action. First, the Hypothalmus gland secretes s substance called CRH that stimulates the pituitary gland. The pituitary secretes the ACTH molecule, which travels to the adrenal gland. The adrenal gland releases cortisol, a hormone that helps keep blood sugar up and gives the body extra energy to act. If you were a cavedweller with rhinos all around, you would be thankful for the boost. If you are an accountant, however, you might become restless and not know how to respond to the chemistry set exploding inside your body.

Other responses also kick into gear. The adrenal glands produce epinephrine that increases heart and breathing rates for better fighting and defending. Blood pressure rises as well, as the legs and arms receive extra blood for more energy. All of this dissipates as the threat is ended.

Today most of us don't face rhinos. Some of us might have bosses who wear on us and never give us a break. If we do, the lingering effects of the stress hormones can be quite damaging. Our memory becomes impaired. The immune system is weakened. High blood pressure and stomach ulcers are common. Skin problems and digestive difficulties also follow.

It is in our best interest to deal with problems as soon as possible, so the adverse side effects have as little opportunity as possible to damage us.

"I told you these things so that

you can have peace in me.

In this world you will have trouble,

but be brave!

I have defeated the world."

JOHN 16:33 NCV

THE CHOICE TO EMBRACE YOUR LIFE

THE BIG LIE: *If I just act as if there is no problem, it will finally go away.*

After my divorce in 2003, I had to face the fact that people would talk about it and reach their own conclusions, and I would never have a chance to let them know my perspective. I hated this part of my life; I just wanted it to go away, but I had to face it. If I was going to heal, I had to face it, accept it, and embrace it.

The "face it" part was difficult enough, but the "embrace it" part was something else entirely. I did not want to embrace it—that would mean making it part of me. It would mean accepting that my identity would always be connected to the word *divorce*. And in embracing that fact, I would move into it rather than away from it and use the experience to help others rather than try to hide it to help myself. I did not want that level of acceptance of the thing I had tried to avoid for so long, but slowly I began to feel differently. Things happened that allowed me to pick up my life as it was and begin to embrace it and all the tough realities that went with it.

We are all messed up, and I have been speaking and writing about being messed up for some time. But with the divorce I had a chance to live it. All of my past struggles were just that—in the past. The divorce was the present, and I had an opportunity to walk through it with others who were struggling with divorce or with some other trauma. Previously, it was all about my college days or high school struggles, but now it was going to be about now. I had told people for years that I was a fellow struggler, but I always left the impression that I had conquered all my struggles and was living at a higher level. Embracing the painful divorce and walking right into it meant that I was truly stepping off any kind of pedestal I had crafted for myself and was going to connect with people in a more authentic and personal way.

I began to believe I could face this and embrace it. I could make it as a divorced man, a broken leader of a ministry, a single father, and a person who has always wanted to communicate truth in a realistic way. I started to tell myself that I could do this and started to believe it. I started to feel that God would be with me and there would be good times ahead.

So I embraced my new identity as a divorced person and began to connect with others in the same situation.

I embraced the circumstances of being a single father and all that goes with that. I embraced the challenge of looking people in the eye and knowing they had questions and doubts. With the help of God I could show them by my actions and by my decisions about the future that I was worthy of their trust. This was not the end of life as I knew it as much as it was the beginning of life as I had never known it.

Tell me in the morning about your love,

because I trust you.

Show me what I should do,

because my prayers go up to you.

LORD, save me from my enemies;

I hide in you.

PSALM 143:8-9 NCV

DAY ONE: *Allow God to work through your situation.*

Joni Eareckson Tada became confined to a wheelchair after diving into a shallow pond and breaking her neck. She is a quadriplegic as a result of one small judgment error. I don't think God ever intended that Joni break her neck. But once she did, He knew He could work with it, and He has done so in a glorious way. Because of Joni's courage in the face of no miraculous healing, many others with illnesses and handicaps have found the courage to continue. They have not given up, because they have seen Joni writing, painting, speaking, singing, and living an amazing life. When you look back on it, you almost think it was meant to be that way from the beginning.

Such examples provided the insight I needed to deal with my own life. Embrace your circumstances, as horrible as they are, and one day you will look back and it will appear it was part of the plan. God can work with anything . . . and He does.

❦

ACT OF HEALING: Develop a habit of taking your problems to God first, before you then try to solve them on your own or before you ask others' advice. Read Psalm 4 for encouragement.

DAY TWO: *Follow Paul's example.*

The apostle Paul wanted to win the world over to the Christian faith, but instead of being free to preach wherever he wanted, he found himself jailed. I don't think God intended for an evil government to imprison the number one proponent of the faith, but if you look back at the story, it almost seems like that is what God meant to happen all along. Paul, sitting there doing jail time, had nothing better to do than write letters. What might have seemed like a waste of time then, now seems like part of a well-designed plan. If you look at how influential Paul is in the church today and how much of the New Testament was written by him, it feels like God meant for Paul to be in jail all along.

❦

ACT OF HEALING: Pray today that your difficulties will be used for good purposes by God and that you will be able to see meaning in them someday even if you can't right now.

DAY THREE: *Let God work with your mistakes.*

Whatever comes along, our mistakes or the mistakes of others, it seems God is there saying, "I can work with that if you will embrace it and allow Me to handle it." I don't know what reality you're facing. I don't know what horrible thing you wish you could just make go away, but I encourage you to allow God to work with it. Don't deny reality or try to cover it up. Embrace it, and embrace all of your life. He can use you greatly, and He can use your situation. Embrace it and allow God to work with it while God is working on you.

⊰⊱

ACT OF HEALING: Read Psalm 25 and look closely for the encouragement in these verses. Then name each problem you are facing and release those problems to God to work with.

DAY FOUR: *Adjust your expectations.*

For most people, embracing their own lives comes down to making a radical adjustment of expectations. If you do not do that, you will always hang on to the life you thought you deserved or wanted. But if you adjust your expectations, you can embrace life as it is and live life to the fullest, and you will discover that the life you have is more meaningful than the life you thought you deserved or wanted.

Perhaps you have been shaking a fist at God because He has not delivered to you the life you wanted. You can adjust your expectations and embrace the life He has given you. You might have expected something close to perfect out of yourself. You could not deliver on that, so adjust your expectations. Accept your own humanity and limitations and allow God to work with you in spite of them.

❁

ACT OF HEALING: List the unfulfilled expectations you had for your life. Pray that God will change your heart and help you embrace what is despite what may never be.

DAY FIVE: *Embrace the abrasive.*

Embracing your life means embracing all of it, including the people who make it difficult. I call these people "grace growers" or "character builders." They are used to help mold us into what God wants us to be. These people who are so tough are actually gifts from God. Like me, you probably can look at the character you have developed and see that it did not get there from people being nice to you. You've developed character because of tough treatment by people who did not have your best interests in mind.

God allows these struggles, and in permitting them He uses them to advance His purposes and His kingdom. David, a man after God's own heart, never would have been the man he was if he hadn't been the victim of Saul's jealousy. Difficult things and difficult people make up the stories of our lives in a way that can honor God.

❧

ACT OF HEALING: Who are the difficult people in your life? Reflect on the ways you have grown by having to deal with these people.

DAY SIX: *Take up your cross.*

Eventually you become grateful that your life turned out the way it did. A tragedy might have been the thing you needed to start living life as God wanted. Drop your anger and bitterness over the way life is, and embrace it.

Luke 9:23–25 tells us to give up what we thought we needed and discover what God has for us: "If anyone would come after me, he must deny himself and take up his cross daily and follow me. For whoever wants to save his life will lose it, but whoever loses his life for me will save it. What good is it for a man to gain the whole world, and yet lose or forfeit his very self?" (NIV). You might be holding on to a life you were never meant to live. Adjust your expectations, embrace the life you have, and discover what God can make of it—mistakes and all.

❁

ACT OF HEALING: Pray today that God will help you release any anger and bitterness you feel because of how your life has turned out. Give it up in order to move into the abundant life God wants for you.

DAY SEVEN: *Don't stand in the way.*

The big lie is that if you just act as if the hard realities are not there, they will go away eventually. This lie is not something you only keep up in your head or down in your heart; this lie becomes a way of life. You live it every day, and it keeps you from a life that is full of meaning, purpose, and connection. You live in denial of who you are, and one day you find that you are living, or attempting to live, someone else's life. Rather than face each day as it is, you are trapped in living each day as you wish it were. In doing that you miss so much of what your life could be.

I want to challenge you not to bide your time and simply hope that whatever you are dealing with will just go away. I challenge you to make your experiences the centerpiece of your life and find a way to use them for God's glory.

❦

ACT OF HEALING: How are you standing in the way of what God is trying to do in your life through the struggle you are facing? Resolve to get out of the way and to let God use your experiences for good in the lives of those around you.

But LORD,

you are our father.

We are like clay,

and you are

the potter;

your hands made us all.

ISAIAH 64:8 NCV

Then Peter came to Jesus

and asked, "Lord, when my

fellow believer sins against me,

how many times must I forgive him?

Should I forgive him

as many as seven times?"

Jesus answered, "I tell you,

you must forgive him

more than seven times.

You must forgive him even if he does

wrong to you seventy-seven times."

MATTHEW 18:21–22 NCV

THE CHOICE TO FORGIVE

THE BIG LIE: *Forgiveness is only for those who deserve it or earn it.*

We live in a world where danger and terror are all around us. Since 9/11 most of us have a little more fear that terror might one day strike our personal world. But something else is much more dangerous than some terrorist who might or might not harm us one day. There is something worse, much worse than that. This danger is worse because it can exist within us. It can affect everything we do and the very person we become. That internal terrorist is called a "justifiable resentment."

Many people carry resentments. Some just seem to have a bad attitude about life and they lean toward resenting everything. They resent paying taxes, paying more than a dollar for a gallon of gas, or being asked by the church to give money to support the new building campaign. They resent the people they live with, not because they live with bad people, but because they've amassed a collection of little things to hold against them.

It makes the "resenters" feel a bit superior, so they hang on to everything they can find. They go through life being negative on anything and everything. These petty resentments are real resentments, real problems, but they are not the type that will kill you.

A *justifiable* resentment is the type of resentment that will kill you. It is not about anything petty. It is about real and horrible mistreatment or abuse. It is about a real-life event that anyone would say was terribly wrong, and almost anyone would tell you that you are justified in feeling the way you do. All the evidence supports your feelings of anger, resentment, bitterness, and unwillingness to forgive. The other person does not deserve forgiveness, and no one wants him or her to have it. That is what I call a justifiable resentment.

Real resentment over real damage by a real person produces a justifiable resentment, and it becomes such a huge part of your life that it feels like a vulture sitting on top of you—a dark and dangerous presence that affects everything you do. It hurts your relationship with God and with others. You will be firmly rooted to your past and to your abuse as long as the justifiable resentment grows within you. It will come to define who you are and limit what you can become.

Believe it or not, you really can be free from justifiable resentment. You can let it go and experience the healing power of forgiveness. You can choose to heal a troubled area of your soul by choosing to walk through a path of forgiveness. And if you take this path, something amazing will happen to you one day.

One day you will awaken and realize that everything in your life has changed. You will sense that you are no longer rooted in your past. You will realize that what once defined your life and your inner thoughts is no longer relevant to how you live your life. You won't forget what happened, but the weight of the past will seem like nothing more than a fly you can just swoosh away. That little fly is nothing compared to the vulture perched atop your soul, talons deeply implanted in your heart. One day you will awaken, the vulture will be gone, and you will be free.

But you are a forgiving God.

You are kind and full of mercy.

You do not become angry quickly,

and you have great love.

So you did not leave them.

NEHEMIAH 9:17 NCV

DAY ONE: *Learn the physiology of forgiveness.*

The psalmist wisely stated that in the guilt of his sin and in the silence and covering it up, his "body wasted away" (Psalm 32:3 NASB). He knew then what science is just now coming to accept. Guilt, resentment, sin, and silence have a physiological impact on a person. They all combine to create an emotionally and physically sick person who misses the best of life because he or she is stuck in the past that cannot be changed.

The physiology of forgiveness works for you to stop the "wasting away" that the psalmist mentioned. When you open up about your own sin and accept God's forgiveness for it, you begin to change your physiology. When you forgive someone else for something they did, the change comes in your "heart"—as in your soul—and also in your "heart"—as in the big red muscle pumping inside your chest.

❋

ACT OF HEALING: List any physical effects you may be experiencing due to unforgiveness or guilt. Ask God to show you the people you need to forgive, and then choose to forgive them.

DAY TWO: *Live as a forgiver.*

Resentment and bitterness cut us off from others and make us suspicious and fearful of relationships. Resentment isolates us and creates a loner mentality. It becomes the ultimate wall between a healthy social network of family, friends, neighbors, community, and us. You shed people when you refuse to forgive. You need to develop a new way of thinking and relating, rather than live a life where you feel entitled to hang on to grudges.

You can choose to live as a forgiver. You can choose to make your whole life work better by incorporating the repeated act of forgiveness into the person you are. If you have created a life where grudges are common and resentment lingers in many of your associations, the choice to forgive is the choice to heal your future and to heal who you are right now. The benefits of forgiveness are too great to live without.

❧

ACT OF HEALING: Reflect on this question: What does it mean to you to forgive someone—not just to accept an apology but to make a choice to forgive (again and again, if needed) and to move on?

DAY THREE: *Don't wait until they ask.*

You must not get hung up on whether or not someone wants to be forgiven or deserves it. If you wait for others to want forgiveness, you might waste your life waiting for something that will never happen. The hardness of another person's heart is not an excuse for you to harden yours. Forgive freely even when the offenders are unaware they hurt you. Forgive even though others deny that your pain is their problem. Give them forgiveness from your heart so your heart can be free.

You don't have to confront someone to be able to forgive them. I think such confrontations often cause more problems than they solve. They immediately put others on the offensive, or at least they're likely to. I think it is better to just forgive the person. Let it go, and get on with your life. If you need to document what happened, write it in your Bible or journal.

❧

ACT OF HEALING: If you have made the choice to forgive someone who has hurt you, write about it in your journal. Declare this the day when you choose to move forward and not look back.

DAY FOUR: *Recognize what Christ did for you.*

A pretty sharp directive is found in Matthew 6:14–15: "If you forgive men when they sin against you, your heavenly Father will also forgive you. But if you do not forgive men their sins, your Father will not forgive your sins" (NIV).

Those verses can be confusing because we also are told in Romans 10:9, "That if you confess with your mouth, "Jesus is Lord," and believe in your heart that God raised him from the dead, you will be saved" (NIV). Matthew 6 seems to indicate that salvation requires more from us than Romans 10 does. Here is what I believe: The only reason you would refuse to forgive others of their sins is because you wouldn't fully grasp what God has done for you or the sins from which He freed you. If you don't believe you are a sinner in need of forgiveness, then you won't forgive others. If you are grateful that God has forgiven you through Christ, then you naturally will extend to others what has been extended to you. If you are holding a grudge, I have to ask if you truly believe and trust in Christ.

❦

ACT OF HEALING: How does Jesus' sacrifice for your sins encourage you to respond to those who have hurt you? Write your response in your journal.

DAY FIVE: *Accept your own need for forgiveness.*

Sometimes it is hard for us to forgive others because we feel so unforgiven ourselves. The Bible says: "Therefore if you bring your gift to the altar, and there remember that your brother has something against you, leave your gift there before the altar and go your way. First be reconciled to your brother and then come and offer your gift" (Matthew 5:23–24 NKJV). This is a direct command to take care of personal business before moving on with the spiritual business at hand. When we do, it is a gift to the other person, but it is also a great gift to ourselves.

I want to beg you to do something in the area of your own need for forgiveness. It could change your life. It could restore a relationship and bring deep healing to both the other person and you.

❧

ACT OF HEALING: On a scale of 1 to 7—with 1 being "completely unforgiven," 4 being "half-forgiven," and 7 being "fully forgiven"—how would you rate your sense of your own forgiveness? Based on your score, what do you need to do about your own need for forgiveness?

ASKING FOR FORGIVENESS
EXAMPLE LETTER ONE

Dear _____,

You are probably surprised to hear from me. It has been a long time.

I am writing because I need to clear my conscience. In the past, when there were situations or conflicts that were hurtful, I sometimes would choose to avoid a person, rather than attempt to resolve the problem.

However, the closer I walk with Jesus, He is showing me that closing doors does not heal relationships. It only temporarily helped me to avoid uncomfortable situations.

Yet God is good. He has forgiven me for all my shortcomings! Now, out of gratitude to Him, I am apologizing to you for my past actions. I am sorry for hurting you.

Please forgive me.

Sincerely,

ASKING FOR FORGIVENESS
EXAMPLE LETTER TWO

Dear _____,

I have been thinking about you a lot. I have been praying for you and hoping that your life is going well.

The reason I have been thinking about you and praying for you is that I have wanted to confess to you that I was so wrong in what I did. I offer no defense and no excuses or rationalizations. I was wrong and I have lived with the guilt and shame ever since.

I wanted you to know that I did not escape unpunished. I have felt the pain of it almost every day.

I am writing to ask for your forgiveness. I can understand why you would not give it. But I wanted you to know that you mean something to me, and I am so sorry for what I did.

Please forgive me.

I will continue to pray for you and hope for your best.

Sincerely,

DAY SIX: *Take the risk and change a life.*

Don't listen to the big lie that forgiveness is only for people who earn it or deserve it. None of us deserves forgiveness. It is a gift of grace from God. He did the unfathomable of taking on our sins and enduring punishment for them. He did what we don't have to do, so we could do what we cannot do. If God has done it for us, we can do it for others. Another person's emotional state or attitude should have nothing to do with our plans to forgive. You never know what a simple request for forgiveness might do for that person.

People's lives have been changed because someone took a risk and asked for forgiveness. The risk becomes the seed of healing in another person's life. You might be the most unlikely candidate to help in the process, but God has a history of using unlikely people to accomplish His goals. Whether you need forgiveness or you need to forgive, making contact and taking a risk will make you a peacemaker and blessed in the eyes of God. Don't wait until someone deserves forgiveness. Forgive anyway, and begin the process right now.

﹡

ACT OF HEALING: What holds you back from forgiving others? Continue in this process of forgiveness by searching yourself and asking God to search you.

DAY SEVEN: *Pull up anchor.*

Resentment, bitterness, and a lack of forgiveness anchor us to a past that cannot be changed. We cannot go back and undo the damage of yesterday, but we can undo the damage it is causing today. We do that with the act of forgiveness. First, we seek God's forgiveness and bathe in its liberating grace. We allow ourselves to be forgiven, and we live as forgiven rather than as guilty and shameful beings. We must clear up our own irresponsibilities by making restitution and seeking to reconcile when it is appropriate. Then we need to offer up to others what we have experienced for ourselves. We uproot our own anchors to the past, and we grab other people's chains to help them pull up their own anchors.

Healing is a choice. The choice to forgive is as big a choice as we can make. It is the often the last choice of those who have been hurt badly. No matter what you have done or what was done to you, I hope you will make the healing choice to forgive.

❧

ACT OF HEALING: Envision yourself pulling up each of the wrongs that anchor you to your past. How can you pull up anchor by making restitution (if appropriate) and by choosing to forgive (always appropriate)?

Lord, you are kind
and forgiving
and have great love
for those who call to you.

PSALM 86:5 NCV

REMBRANDT'S PRODIGAL

✻

Some years back I was in Toronto, Canada, listening to Henry Nouwen speak. He was amazing as he spoke on the Prodigal Son. Most people know the story of the boy who demanded his half of the inheritance and then squandered it all, only to find himself living among pigs and eating the pigs' diet of husks and other scraps. In a great moment of insight he realized that his father's servants ate better, so he made his way humbly back home to ask to serve and experience good food and a secure place to live. When he came up over the hill, there was his father, looking off in the distance as if he had been waiting all along. He greeted the boy and welcomed him back into the family by placing a ring on his finger and throwing a major celebration.

It is interesting to note that the boy had already taken his half of everything. When he returned his expectations were few, but his father placed a ring on his finger symbolizing that he was now entitled to half again. He had been accepted back with full status as son.

No wonder the elder brother was angry. He was now down to a fourth of the original inheritance. Rather than be grateful for that and for the redemption of his brother, he was full of anger and resentment. The story is rich with symbolism and representation. The father represents God's feelings and actions toward us. The prodigal represents all of us who rebel and go our separate ways. The elder brother represents our judgmental ways of dealing with those who have been caught up in sin and find their way back to our churches.

That night Henry Nouwen concluded his talk by handing out prints of a painting by Rembrandt of the moment when the father welcomed the prodigal son back home. "The Return of the Prodigal Son" is a painting of the boy kneeling before the father, and the father with his arms around the boy, his hands resting on the boy's back. If you look closely at the painting you see that one of the hands is strong and full of power, obviously painted from the model of a man who was full of power and strength. If you look closely at the other hand, though, you discover something quite amazing. The other hand is smaller, softer, gentler. Rembrandt used a female to model for the second hand. That second hand represents the gentle grace that God possesses and shares with us. It is the hand of a God so loving that He would send His perfect Son to suffer and die for all of His prodigal children. When we understand the magnitude of that, we are willing to extend that same forgiveness to others. The way I read Matthew 6, not only does our life here on earth depend on forgiveness, our eternal life depends on it also.

So we can be sure when we say,

"I will not be afraid,

because the Lord is my helper.

People can't do anything to me."

HEBREWS 13:6 NCV

THE CHOICE TO RISK YOUR LIFE

THE BIG LIE: *I Must Protect Myself from More Pain*

The path of healing takes you through the depths of your feelings, grief, forgiveness, and the embracing of all of your life. When areas aren't healing, you seek out and obtain the treatment that you need. You choose to heal, and with each choice you allow God's healing grace to replace the sick parts of your soul. You find your life again, or perhaps for the first time. As you grow, you reach a point where you either move forward or you remain stagnant and miss your life. You either cower in fear to protect yourself, or you take a leap of faith propelled by courage—you begin to risk.

If you have suffered one disease, you risk getting another one. If you have been hurt by a man, you put yourself at risk by having a relationship with another one. If you have been so riddled with fear that you have confined yourself to your neighborhood or house or just your room, you take a risk and get outside of the walls you have built to protect yourself. Those walls have not protected you; rather, they have infected you with soul rot because you ceased to live while locked behind them.

Life without risk is not much of a life. I know young men who inherited a lot of money and had all the comforts and securities you could possibly ask for. They had it all but lived with no fire in the belly because there was nothing to burn. Because their lives were so predictable and comfortable and risk free, they missed becoming the men they could have been.

Predictability really can chain us to old things and prevent us from moving toward the new. Comfort can encase us in a womb we should have outgrown but still retreat into. We must give up the chains of predictability and the womb of comfort and jump out there and take a risk if we are to truly live.

Risk is a choice to heal because it stretches some of the scar tissue and prevents us from being restrained by the energy. Just like a burn patient who must painfully move the scarred limbs to stretch the skin, we must do the same with our souls. We must stretch into what is not comfortable, so that we do not confine ourselves to what is comfortable. That stretching comes from risk.

We risk connecting, because if we don't then parts of us will die in isolation. We must risk loving again, because if we don't we will become bitter and isolated. We risk succeeding, knowing that it might prove to be a failure and we might look inadequate. If we do not risk, however, we will live a horrible life of boredom and loneliness convincing ourselves we are okay as we mark time toward a miserable end. It does not have to be that way if we will choose to take a risk.

With God's power working in us,

God can do much, much more

than anything we can ask or imagine.

EPHESIANS 3:20 NCV

DAY ONE: *Take risks.*

Have you stopped to think of what you might be missing because you are unwilling to risk? Perhaps it is a relationship with an amazing person. Perhaps it is being on a mission where lives are changed forever. Maybe it is being in a group where you share your life and find hope and encouragement. There are so many things you might miss if you are unwilling to take a risk.

I understand the security that comes from everything remaining the same, but predictability can become a god. You may choose to live your life in a predictable way instead of seeking what God would have you to do. There may be a new life out there waiting for you if you are willing to take a risk.

❊

ACT OF HEALING: Stop to assess your readiness for taking risks. When was the last time you took a real risk? Are you willing to do so now? What keeps you from taking more healthy risks in your life?

DAY TWO: *Implement the buddy system.*

If you are so out of your comfort zone you think you might not ever be able to risk again, you need to get a buddy. You need to find someone who has been through what you have been through and made it out the other side. You can bolster your own confidence by relying on the strength of two rather than one. Think about people you know who could help you by going to a meeting with you or even going on a date. Think of different areas where a buddy might help you live again, and write down those ideas. If you don't know of anyone, then your pastor or recovery group might be able to help you find someone. It might be a little embarrassing to ask for help getting out of your comfort zone, but the world you are going to live in is worth the risk—and so is the reward.

※

ACT OF HEALING: Read Ecclesiastes 4:10–12. As hard as it might be, find someone to partner with you in risk-taking. You might be surprised at the result!

DAY THREE: *Let love drive out your fear.*

"There is no fear in love. But perfect love drives out fear, because fear has to do with punishment. The one who fears is not made perfect in love" (1 John 4:18 NIV). If you have a riskless nature, it may be because you have a loveless nature. Your love relationship with God might be all messed up. You might be so afraid that He will punish you that you are unwilling to enjoy your life by living it to the fullest and using it to serve others. If you live in fear of punishment rather than in the confidence of God's love, it is no wonder that you don't want to risk. You must have God's love, God's Spirit, and God's power if you are to conquer your fears and move into risking your life.

❀

ACT OF HEALING: Look up Psalm 103:8, Romans 8:38-39, and 1 John 3:1. Write them out in your journal, and refer to them to remind yourself that you don't need to fear anything.

DAY FOUR: *Release your grip.*

If you are holding on way too tight, let go. I am hopeful that you can release your grip and allow God to guide you into some situations that may seem scary for you alone, but for you and God together they hold no downside at all. God said, "Never will I leave you, never will I forsake you!" (Hebrews 13:5 NIV).

God will never forsake you. Nothing you can do will drive God away. He will never leave you. God loves you and will be there to help you pick up the pieces and put them back together as something far more beautiful than the original. God created you and will always be there for you. If God is for you in that way, who could possibly be against you and win? God loves you. God is there for you, and you need have no fear of today or of what tomorrow might bring.

❧

ACT OF HEALING: What does it mean that God will never leave you or forsake you? How does God's promise relate to the specific fears you have in your life? Throughout the day, remind yourself that God is with you.

DAY FIVE: *Share Christ's suffering.*

You've used many excuses to play it safe. They have worked well for you in your goal to avoid risk, but they have not worked well for you in living a great life. To live a great life you must have risk. You cannot love unless you risk. You cannot connect without risk. Loving, caring, and connecting—those vital elements give life meaning and purpose, and they are great reasons to risk.

You also can't serve without risking. But when you serve, you serve Christ. You do for Christ what you do for another. When you serve and are not loved for it, but instead are rejected, you share in the sufferings of Jesus. You fellowship with Christ through your rejection because almost all of His life was filled with rejection. That fellowship with Christ is a powerful healer that cannot be experienced unless you are willing to take some risks.

❈

ACT OF HEALING: Begin reading through one of the four Gospels and note how often Jesus faced rejection. Take comfort in the knowledge that you share in His sufferings when you take risks.

DAY SIX: *Cast your anxiety on God.*

The great preacher Charles Haddon Spurgeon said, "Anxiety does not empty tomorrow of its sorrows but only empties today of its strength." You cannot lead a healed life in anxiety. It will rob you of the strength you need today. It will steal from you the tomorrow you were born to enjoy.

The answer for those who need healing from a risk-adverse life is found in 1 Peter 5:7: "Cast all your anxiety on him because he cares for you" (NIV) Do that right now. You can trust that God cares for you. It is worth the risk to tell God that you give Him all your fears and you are ready to ride out your life on the front seat of the first car of the rollercoaster, healed in excited anticipation of what might be around the next turn.

✥

ACT OF HEALING: Write out what you fear. Write out what you have held onto for yourself and what you need to surrender to God.

DAY SEVEN: *Choose to take a risk.*

You are going to be hurt and you cannot do anything to prevent it, but what you *can* do is trust God each time a hurt comes along. Trust that while you don't have the power to protect yourself, He has the power to turn every hurt into something that improves who you are and glorifies Him. You will never protect yourself from all the hurt, but you will protect yourself from missing the life God intended when you make the choice to risk.

Healing is a choice. It is God's choice, but many times we stand in the way of what God wants for us. Our stubbornness often prevents us from looking at the reality of our lives, but God challenges us to make choices that heal. No choice is more difficult than the choice to risk. My hat is off to all of you who will make that choice today. Blessings of God be upon you for your amazing courage.

❦

ACT OF HEALING: What risk have you been avoiding? Take action toward a healing risk today.

God did not give us

a spirit that makes us afraid

but a spirit of power

and love and self-control.

2 TIMOTHY 1:7 NCV

When we have the opportunity
to help anyone, we should do it.

But we should

give special attention

to those who are

in the family of believers.

GALATIANS 6:10 NCV

THE CHOICE TO SERVE

THE BIG LIE: *Until I am completely healed and strong there is no place for me to serve God.*

Most people are familiar with a wonderful story in the Book of Judges about a man named Gideon. Two things are well known about the story. One is his use of a fleece to see if God was really with him. The other is his great battle victory against what seemed to be insurmountable odds. However, the best part of the story for me is found in Judges 6:11–16:

> One day the angel of God came and sat down under the oak in Ophrah that belonged to Joash the Abiezrite, whose son Gideon was threshing wheat in the winepress, out of sight of the Midianites.
>
> The angel of God appeared to him and said, "God is with you, O mighty warrior!"
>
> Gideon replied, "With me, my master? If God is with us, why has all this happened to us? Where are all the miracle-wonders our parents and grandparents told us about, telling us, 'Didn't God deliver us from

Egypt?' The fact is, God has nothing to do with us—
he has turned us over to Midian."

But God faced him directly: "Go in this strength that is
yours. Save Israel from Midian. Haven't I just sent you?"

Gideon said to him, "Me, my master? How and with
what could I ever save Israel? Look at me. My clan's the
weakest in Manasseh and I'm the runt of the litter."

God said to him, "I'll be with you. Believe me, you'll
defeat Midian as one man." (MSG)

Even if Gideon had been a horrible warrior I would have
still loved this story. It points out two amazing things about
God. First, Gideon had his doubts about God because of the
circumstances around him. The Midianites were mistreating
the Israelites, and Gideon was not happy about it. When God
comes to him, Gideon is not much of a believer. He has heard
what God has done in the past, but he has seen nothing
like the miracles that freed the Israelites from Egypt.
However, if Gideon will do as he is told and serve God in
the way God needs him to serve, he will become part of one
of the greatest miracles ever told.

You—right now in the midst of your difficult circumstances
—might doubt whether or not God exists or is involved in
your life. It might feel as if God either is not in heaven or
doesn't care about you. You might feel so weak that you
cannot relate to a powerful God who doesn't seem to be
doing anything in your life. But just as God was with Gideon,

even though Gideon was not aware of God or could not feel God's presence, God is with you and wants to use you.

God wants you to serve Him. This is the second amazing thing in this part of Gideon's story. God has a purpose for your life. God wants you to go after that purpose and be used by Him for the benefit of His kingdom. God will take you and use you even if you get up and go along with Him kicking and screaming like a big baby. Kick and scream, but move toward the place where God wants you. Doubt God's presence, but risk enough to trust in what you do not see. At the height of your pain or abuse or neglect it might not have seemed that God was there or involved. It certainly did not seem that way to Gideon, but God was there and God was planning all along to use Gideon, just as God has planned all along to use you, if you will let Him.

DAY ONE: *Reflect on your story.*

If you believe the Bible to be true, the story of Gideon has to have an impact on your life. If you believe God speaks to us through His Word, surely you believe He has used this story to help you overcome any excuse you might have for not serving Him. Gideon's story is God choosing a weak man from a weak clan to lead a weak army to defeat a mighty foe. What is your story? If someone one day would write a Third Testament and your story was in it, what would it say? Would it be a great story of victory against the greatest of odds? Would it be a story of how you refused to allow any excuse to keep you from living out your purpose and calling from God? I am praying as I write that as you will choose to remove any excuse from your life that keeps you from serving God.

❧

ACT OF HEALING: Write an outline of your life story. What themes do you see? What would you like the outcome to be? How might God use the events of your past for good?

DAY TWO: *Give up your excuses.*

What are your excuses for not serving God?

Are you weak? Perfect. When lives are changed and people are transformed, God will get double glory because of the result.

Are you wounded? Perfect. When God uses a wounded person to heal someone else, not only will He get the glory for the result in the life of the once-sick, but He also will be glorified when people see how your assistance of others fuels a healing process in you.

Are you untalented? Perfect. God does not need talent. All God needs is willingness, and He takes that willingness and weaves it into a miracle.

Right now I am inviting you to surrender your excuses and serve God. Your situation could not be any worse than Gideon's, and your miracle will be no less if you move out of your old life and into God's purpose for you. Give up any excuse that keeps you stagnant and self-absorbed and pick up your life and serve. When you do, you will be astounded at the healing that will come.

❧

ACT OF HEALING: Make a list of the excuses you have used to avoid serving God.

DAY THREE: *Come alive.*

When you pick up your life and serve, you find a new life. You come alive in ways you never dreamed. Have you made every healing choice except for the one choice to serve God? If so, you are not fully aware of what your life can be. You should be excited about that. If you have ever been so dull and dead that you wondered, "Is this all there is?" be encouraged. This is not all there is. This life is not just about how hurt you feel or about how badly you have been treated. This life is about how God uses bad people— who feel bad because they have been treated badly—to do good things for Him. All of the previous choices help to bring you here, a place of service. All the choices are weak and shallow if they do not lead you to this place and motivate you to reach out to others to do whatever you can. All He asks is that you give a little to others of what He has given to you.

❈

ACT OF HEALING: What experiences have you had that might help someone else? Whom do you desire to help? Make a list of the possibilities. Find a way this week to give a little to others of what God has given to you.

DAY FOUR: *Comfort others.*

Second Corinthians 1:4 says, "He comforts us in all our troubles so that we can comfort others. When others are troubled, we will be able to give them the same comfort God has given us" (NLT). Now, you might be thinking you have not been given enough comfort yet. You might tell both yourself and God that you want to serve, but serving just doesn't feel right because you don't feel right. You may tell yourself that lie until the day you die. I am giving you a personal invitation to throw that excuse away. Take whatever comfort God has given you and use it. You might not have much insight yet, but some people have none. Use what little you have to reach out and help others.

❧

ACT OF HEALING: Think of a way in which you can use your healing journey to help someone else who is not as far along. How might you be able to share what you have learned?

DAY FIVE: *Find your secret powers.*

Romans 12 is one place we learn about the spiritual gifts that I call secret powers. Other gifts are outlined in 1 Corinthians 12. We learn that some people have a gift to declare God's truth in such a way that people turn from their old ways and start new lives. Some are called to serve others with all of their lives, such as being an assistant to a missionary or building houses for the homeless. You might have the gift of teaching and are able to organize and present your thoughts in such a way that people truly learn God's Word and His principles. You might be an encourager and always seem to have the words that will cheer up others or point out the best in the worst of situations. There are people who have the gift of giving. There also is the gift of giving wise advice, the supernatural ability to know what God would say to a person, and many, many more wonderful powers that you've been given to use.

※

ACT OF HEALING: Read Romans 12. Which gifts do you *think* you have? Which gifts do you *know* you have? How might you use these gifts?

DAY SIX: *Recognize Satan's goal.*

Satan is your enemy, and he does not want you to heal. He rebelled against the kingdom of God, and he certainly does not want you going around helping build it. He will trap you in the lie that you are not ready to serve. If he has his way you will never be ready, you will never feel ready, and you will never do anything helpful or unselfish with your life. He will get you to believe: "Until I am completely healed and strong there is no place for me to serve God." If you believe your gifts and talents are not strong enough or good enough, then Satan has you right where he wants you. If you think the mistakes you've made disqualify you from helping others, then your stagnant life will glorify Satan, not God.

Do not listen to the lies that rob you of your life. Make the healing choice to reach out and discover how God can use you to serve others.

❄

ACT OF HEALING: List the lies that Satan is telling you about why you are not ready to serve the Lord. Respond to each lie with truth from God's Word about who you are in Christ.

DAY SEVEN: *Use what you have.*

In the twenty-fifth chapter of Matthew is a fascinating passage that expresses the heart of God when it comes to the issue of using what we have to serve others to the best of our abilities. If you read the entire chapter, you plainly see that God expects those who have been given a lot of talents to use them. God also expects those who don't have many talents to use what they do have. He expects us to use what we have in the best way possible.

God calls us to serve. He delivers deeper healing into our souls when we get out of the way and move toward others in humble service. He wants our lives to be inconvenienced for others. He wants our days to be cluttered with untidy people who could use our gifts. He wants us to go without so others can have. God is interested in us sharing our lives in humble service. When we do, we discover what we are here for. We find fulfillment when we live out that calling and purpose.

✿

ACT OF HEALING: Read Matthew 25. Today, allow yourself to be inconvenienced for another person.

Let each of us

please our neighbors

for their good,

to help them

be stronger in faith.

ROMANS 15:2 NCV

RENOIR AND MATISSE

Two famous French painters, Renoir and Matisse, were good friends and spent time sharing a portion of their lives with each other. They enjoyed each other's company as they had the common bond of love of color, beauty, and painting. While Matisse painted freely with minimal health concerns, Renoir developed a serious case of arthritis. It was so debilitating as it progressed that he was almost completely paralyzed by it. No matter how severe the pain, no matter how difficult that stroke, he continued to paint. Each brushstroke sent a streak of pain through him. He would wince and jerk as he applied the color to the canvas.

Matisse watched his friend with great concern and passion. He was mystified by the dedication and commitment that led to creating at such a painful level of personal sacrifice. One day he asked Renoir why he continued to paint with such distressing effort. Renoir replied, "Because the beauty remains: the pain passes." What a beautiful picture to all of us who are struggling in painful times.

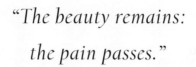

"The beauty remains:

the pain passes."

We have freedom now,

because Christ made us free.

So stand strong.

Do not change and go back

into the slavery of the law.

GALATIANS 5:1 NCV

THE CHOICE TO PERSEVERE

THE BIG LIE: *There is no hope for me.*

As you look at your life, it might not make a lot of sense. You have some ideas about how it all could work so much better, but God doesn't seem to consider or implement your plans. When things seem so clear to you, it is difficult to sit back and allow God to work in your life, but that is exactly what God wants you to do. Your way of doing things is not His way. What looks perfectly right and normal to you is anything but that to Him. What God unfolds and the way He does it might seem foolish and even ridiculous to you, but trust God anyway.

First Corinthians 1:25–29 gives some insight into this. God's "foolish" plan is far wiser than the wisest of human plans, and God's weakness is far stronger than the greatest of human strength:

> *Remember, dear brothers and sisters, that few of you were wise in the world's eyes, or powerful, or wealthy when God called you.*
>
> *Instead, God deliberately chose things the world considers foolish in order to shame those who think they are wise. And he chose those who are powerless to shame those who are powerful.*

God chose things despised by the world, things counted as
nothing at all, and used them to bring to nothing what the
world considers important, so that no one can ever boast in
the presence of God (NLT).

So what does this mean to you? It means that if your
circumstances make no sense to you or to those around you,
perfect. If you cannot see any way out of your mess under
your own power, perfect. If what looks wise and smart to
you is not exactly what God seems to be doing, perfect. God
has been making foolish things work for His good since the
beginning of time. So don't give in to hopelessness; give in
to God's miraculous plan, and allow Him to unfold that
plan right before your eyes.

My question to you is one of trust. Will you trust Him?
Will you trust Him enough to hang on one more day? Will
you trust Him enough to make your foolish circumstances
an example of how He can make the best of the worst
situations? Will you trust Him enough to make the healing
choice to persevere? Will you trust Him enough to live for
Him even when healing is delayed? Will you trust Him
enough to promote the healing of others even while you
make choices for your own healing? Before you can heal,
you have to answer the question of trust.

I beg you to trust Him enough to persevere.

DAY ONE: *Choose to hang on.*

You are wonderfully made, according to Psalm 139. Your life is full of wonder and meaning and value placed there by God. Any feeling otherwise is implanted in you by the evil one. John 10:10 clearly lays out what Satan has done to you and what Christ wants to do for you: "The thief comes only to steal and kill and destroy; I came that you might have life, and have it abundantly" (NASB).

Hebrews 10:36 says, "You need to persevere so that when you have done the will of God, you will receive what he has promised" (NIV). Another translation says that what He has promised is the crown of life. Notice that the verse does not say that you need to be perfect; you just need to hold on and persevere.

I hope you will decide to persevere so that you can see all of the wonder that God can bring from your life. Ask God to come alongside you and help you in ways you never dreamed you could be helped.

❦

ACT OF HEALING: If you need help persevering, call (800) NEW-LIFE to talk to someone who can walk alongside you.

DAY TWO: *Have realistic expectations.*

The more realistic your expectations are about your tough reality, the easier it will be to develop a life that is fulfilling as you walk out of your destructive ways and into the healing ways of God. Don't let unrealistic expectations cause you more frustrations that lead to giving up. Do not give up. God is with you and wants to grow your character. A quick fix or instant solution does not grow you. Healing your soul from the inside out takes work and time. Character is never instant, and God often uses our circumstances to build it within us. Too often people give up on God just before the evidence of His work shows up. Don't let that be you. Continue to persevere—no matter how tough a bind you are in. Do not ever give up. No matter what, let this be the day you decide to continue one more day.

❦

ACT OF HEALING: What quick fixes have you tried? What unrealistic expectations have disappointed you? Set aside those things today, and focus on the hard work of healing.

DAY THREE: *Share your doubts with God.*

God can handle your doubts in the bad times. He knows you and He knows human nature at large. Your doubts are not unexpected, so share your doubts with Him. Doubt all you want, but don't give up. Question everything about your faith, but don't stop moving toward God while the questions are being answered. Persevere. Carry on. Move forward. Do all this as you continue to move toward a closer relationship with God.

Life is not easy. It is hard and God knows that. He hurts with you and weeps with you. Hold on to Him because He is holding on to you. Don't let your doubts rob you of His love. Don't let your questions destroy your relationship with the God of the universe. He can handle the questions and the doubts. Just don't use questions and doubts as an excuse to stop persevering.

❧

ACT OF HEALING: Tell God what doubts have been robbing you of His love. Release those doubts to God and accept His love for you.

DAY FOUR: *Be confident of the outcome.*

Most of us realize that for a field to bring forth a bountiful harvest, the sod must be broken and the fields plowed up. Without the crumbling of the clods into fine rich soil, it would not yield much of a crop. We have no problem understanding that a breaking leads to the fulfillment of that field.

Yet we fight accepting that for ourselves. We are a field and God needs to do some plowing. If we allow Him, He will take the breaking of one lowly substance and transform it into the making of a great life for you. Romans 8:28 tells us that "in all things God works for the good of those who love Him, who are called according to his purpose" (NIV).

No matter what you are going through, it is going to be okay. In fact, it is going to be more than okay. If you persevere with God, through God's power He will make it good for you.

❦

ACT OF HEALING: Are there other times in your life when God used a difficulty for a good purpose? Have you seen Him do this in the life of a friend? Allow these examples to give you hope and courage now.

DAY FIVE: *Believe there is hope for you.*

Your life is like a river, full of mystery, power, and movement. It looks predictable, but below the surface are wild currents that can take you places you might not want to go. You could be out on that river, paddling with all your might upstream. You have exhausted all your earthly power to fight the current to get someplace you believed held the key to your happiness. You have paddled and paddled along that stream. And after all that exhausting work, you are no closer to the life you've always wanted.

I ask you to stop the paddling that saps you of your strength and proves that you do not have it in you to fix your life yourself. Give up on your own strength, and start to move with God's power and strength. Then you will find tremendous hope. There is hope for you, if you will just persevere long enough to find it.

§

ACT OF HEALING: In what ways have you been relying on your own strength? In what ways have you given up hope? Pray to release your life to God's strength so that you may discover the true hope He offers.

DAY SIX: *Surrender to God.*

If you are tired of trying and want to give up, it makes perfect sense. Trying harder does not help a situation. If it did, you would have helped yourself long ago. You cannot continue to run your life and expect to improve your situation under your own power, but you can persevere under the power of God. You have to surrender to Him before you can experience that power.

Surrender to God; let Him do for you what you cannot do for yourself. Give up your ways and invite His ways. Ask for His strength and power, and He will gladly give it to you. Fall back into His arms. Fully give your life to Him. Trust that He is real, and watch Him show you that He is. Watch Him do through you and your pain things that never would have been accomplished otherwise. Do not give up in the midst of the suffering.

❦

ACT OF HEALING: Spend some time praying that God will help you fully surrender to Him and to the ways He wants to use your suffering for good.

DAY SEVEN: *Let God create beauty from your ashes.*

I believe God will create beauty from your ashes. Something of great value will emerge out of your pain. And one day that pain is going to go away forever. You won't feel the pain anymore, but you will be able to look back on your life and know you made a difference. Replacing that pain will be a sense of fulfillment and purpose. Allow God time to bring the beauty that only He can create from a troubled and difficult life. There is beauty to be created from the painful episodes of your life.

If your life is riddled with pain, suffering, and struggle, please do not give up. Surrender and persevere. Let go while you hang on. Never stop believing. Hang on to your God. Hang on to your faith, and hang on to your life. Make the healing choice to persevere, and do whatever you have to do to hang on one more day.

❁

ACT OF HEALING: Reflect upon what you have learned over the past ten weeks of your healing journey. How have you changed and grown? Where are you going?

If he stumbles,

he will not fall,

because the LORD

holds his hand.

PSALM 37:24 NCV

40-DAY CHALLENGE

FIVE MINUTES A DAY...
that could change the rest of your day
FORTY DAYS...
that could change your life forever.

This challenge will:

- ⊰ *implant in your heart and soul the words you need to persevere on the path to healing.*

- ⊰ *change the way you think about yourself.*

- ⊰ *change the way you think about life.*

Read the following prayer and affirmation every morning for forty days.

PRAYER

Lord, I am broken and hurting due to the brokenness of others and mistakes of my own. Please use Your powers to heal me and give me courage to make the choices I need to make to allow Your healing in my life. Forgive me for standing in Your way of healing for me. Thank You for allowing my past to end one second ago, and my future to begin right now in this moment with You.

AFFIRMATION

TODAY I CHOOSE TO HEAL

Today, I choose to heal.

My healing begins right now in this moment.

I am no longer bound by my sick past.

There is healing in my future.

For the next twenty-four hours I choose to live free and heal.

I choose to let go of past hurts that I cannot undo.

I choose to forgive myself for wrong choices in the past.

Today I will dwell on what is good and right, not on the darkness I have experienced or the darkness others invite me to live.

Today I will live beyond myself and live for God.

On this day I will choose to feel my life rather than live in denial.

I will not medicate away my pain, sorrow, or anxiety.

I will allow each negative feeling to lead me to greater depths of healing.

I will not drown out or ignore my negative emotions.

I will work through these feelings and move out of them.

I will not project them onto those around me.

When I am unaware of what choice to make next, I will choose to do the next right thing.

Today I will not hide or run away.

I will connect with those who love me and with those who need my love.

Throughout this day I will stay connected to God and ask Him to guide me and lead me.

Today will be an adventure for me.

I will take a risk and enjoy the unpredictable.

I will not be governed by my fears.

I will choose to do something uncomfortable that might lead me to know the truth about myself or live life to the fullest.

I will not lie to myself today.

I will seek the truth and will ask for help when I need it.

Today I will reestablish some boundaries that will protect me from unhealthy people and unhealthy situations.

I will tear down some walls that are keeping some wonderful people from knowing me and loving me.

If there is some ungrieved loss, I will grieve it as much as I can today, and then put it away.

Today I will choose reality and embrace it.

I will accept my life and pick up my life right where it is.

I refuse to wallow in self-pity.

I will not focus on what I do not have or what might have been.

On this day I will not give up.

No matter how difficult the struggle, I choose to preserve.

I will not let any excuse be strong enough to derail my path to healing.

I will never give up or give in to an old life that did not serve me well.

I will allow no one to discourage me.

Today I will heal and rely on God to deliver it through the choices I make.

Today I will allow God to control my life and each choice I make, I will make with God in mind and love in my heart.

On this day, I choose healing.

I will do what I can do to heal and accept the limitations God has placed before me.

I will see every limitation I encounter as an invitation by God to do for me what I cannot do for myself.

I will accept that healing is sometimes slow and delayed and will grow in character in the meantime.

Today I will step outside myself and serve others.

I will find a need and fill it.

I will find the hurt of another and help heal it.

I will not become self-absorbed or filled with self-obsession.

I will reach out to someone in need and do what I can to meet that need.

Today I will ask for God's help to live out His purpose.

Today I will live for God and not myself.

Today, I choose to live.

Today, I choose to love.

Today, I choose to heal.

Final Thoughts

Right now you hold your future in your hand. This very second is the beginning of the future you choose. You can choose a future that is burdened by an unresolved past that clouds every day with sickness and confusion. You can choose to numb your pain with all of the defective and deficient ways you have used for years. Or you can choose a different future right now. You can ask God to come into your life in a new way. You can choose to live to please God and not yourself. You can choose to live in His promises for healing rather than in your history of brokenness. Your future is your choice. No one can take that from you.

There will be some difficult times ahead of you. You can choose to be shocked by those or you can choose right now to accept difficulty and pain and struggle as a part of life. You can choose to prepare yourself for those difficult times ahead by healing the difficult times you have experienced in the past. Today is your day and you can use it to build the future you always desired. You can make a difference in this world. You are not the exception. Your body might not heal but your soul can. Your mind may always be a little off center, but your soul can be centered on God's healing grace.

I am begging you as a brother who loves you to not let anything stand in your way of healing. Let no man rob you of your joy. Let no woman take away the peace that is so divine it is difficult to understand. No excuse is good enough to lead a life less than you were called to by God. Heal through God's power. Believe that He loves you and wants to help you out of your struggles. Accept the reality of pain, but invite God to use it to help you and help others. I beg you to make one healing choice today so that someday you will be inviting someone else to also walk the healing path. I am asking you to give up your life as you know it so that you can find your life as God knows it. Take hold of your future today and make the choices that will lead to your healing.

"I will give peace,

real peace, to those far and near,

and I will heal them,"

says the LORD.

ISAIAH 57:19 NCV

About the Author
& About New Life

Stephen Arterburn is the founder and chairman of New Life Clinics, the largest provider of Christian counseling and treatment throughout the United States and Canada, and he is also the host of the daily *New Life Live!* national radio program heard on over one hundred outlets. Creator of the Women of Faith® Conferences and the best-selling author of more than thirty books, including *Every Man's Battle*, Mr. Arterburn has appeared on numerous nationally televised talk shows and has been featured in publications such as *The New York Times*, *USA Today*, *TIME*, and *Reader's Digest*.

For more information, visit www.newlife.com or call 1-800-NEW-LIFE.

HEALING IS A CHOICE

Do you WANT to be well?

If your answer is "yes!" then these additional resources from Steve Arterburn can help.

HEALING IS A CHOICE: *10 Decisions That Will Transform Your Life and 10 Lies That Can Prevent You From Making Them*

Healing on all levels—spiritual, emotional, mental, and physical—is a miraculous gift from God; but it is a function of our own decisions and beliefs as well. When we make the right choices and reject the lies, we can find the way to wholeness again.

ISBN 0-7852-1226-4 $22.99

HEALING IS A CHOICE WORKBOOK:
This workbook will help those who struggle from self-inflicted bondage so they can experience the healing that is available from God.

ISBN 1-4185-0194-8 17.99

HEALING IS A CHOICE GROUP STUDY KIT:
This curriculum explores 10 choices to make on the path toward healing. Each kit includes *Healing is a Choice*, a workbook, a facilitator's guide, an instructional DVD, and a CD-ROM.

ISBN 1-4185-0552-8 $79.99

www.HealingisaChoice.org

"He heals the broken-hearted, binding up their wounds."

PSALM 147:3

Trust the LORD with all your heart,

and don't depend on your own understanding.

Remember the LORD in all you do,

and he will give you success.

Don't depend on your own wisdom.

Respect the LORD and refuse to do wrong.

Then your body will be healthy,

and your bones will be strong.

PROVERBS 3:5-8 NCV